Letters

you

will

never

read

Copyright © 2024 Hanna Shebar
Cover design and illustrations © Hanna Shebar

All rights reserved.
No part of this book may be used or reproduced in any manner whatsoever without written permission except in the prints in the context of reviews.

ISBN: 978-1-7378977-5-0

Also by Hanna Shebar

POETRY

50 Quotes To Fall In Love With Yourself

356 Daily Reminders

FICTION

Happily Never After

hanna shebar

Letters you will never read

poems

To the memory of those we have loved and lost.
And to my papa, I hope you can see me from heaven.

CONTENTS

behind the pages	5
I *grief*	9
II *healing*	33
III *moving on*	53

Tomorrow is never a guarantee.
Get the best out of every second.
Appreciate the beauty around, pursue your
passions and cherish the relationships you have.
Life is a collection of moments,
and how you spend them defines your journey.

— Hanna Shebar

BEHIND THE PAGES

When I was in first grade, my teacher asked who I wanted to be when I grew up. Without hesitation, I replied that I wanted to be the president of Ukraine.
While other kids dreamed of becoming doctors, policemen, or teachers, I craved something different and edgy, even at six years old. But my aspiration to become president was genuine. Growing up, I often heard my parents lament the corruption in our government. I believed I could do better—I could change our country.

I consider myself incredibly privileged. I come from a family that supports my individuality and creativity. The people who believed in me and continue to do so are the greatest blessing I could ask for. When I told my grandpa after school that I thought I would be president one day, he responded, "Well, that would be amazing—to have a first female president!"

I was cheered for and supported throughout my life. My mom is my number one fan. Some may say we are both delusional, but if you ask me, you have to be a little delusional to achieve great things. You must believe in the possibility of your dreams to turn them into reality.

In my twenties, I learned I am neurodivergent. That discovery put many things into perspective. Looking back, it seems obvious that I've always had these traits—I can't believe my parents and teachers didn't catch on earlier.

In school, I excelled only in Ukrainian, English, literature, and history. Everything else bored me. Yet, I can't say I was bad at school.

Math and physics weren't my strong points, but I still managed decent grades considering I didn't study half the subjects.
In music school, however, I was at the top of my class. I absorbed everything my teacher taught us and enjoyed every moment of learning. It was a stark contrast to regular school, where I was bullied—not just by kids who teased me for my unconventional fashion choices and interests, but also by some teachers.
This was the state of education in post-Soviet Ukraine.

I always enjoyed writing and believed I had a way with words, but my russian language teacher often discouraged me. My grammar in the three languages I speak was never great, and perhaps my ADHD contributed to that. As a kid, I didn't understand this and felt inferior to my classmates. I remember consistently receiving A's for the content of my essays but C's or D's for grammar.

At 12, I became passionate about writing. After discovering *Pride and Prejudice* by Jane Austin, I started writing my own book. Yet even then, I couldn't picture myself as a professional writer.
It was later, that I decided I wanted to be a journalist. I felt I could make a difference, which had always been a secret goal of mine. In eighth grade, however, I got into YouTube, where I began writing, filming, and editing short films. By ninth grade, I realized this was something I wanted to pursue professionally.

By that time, three of my grandparents had passed away, and the only one I had in my corner was my mom. My father wanted me to follow in the family's footsteps and become a lawyer like him, his father before him, and my mom. I had a different plan. I wanted to be a storyteller—to write and direct films.

He didn't approve. The idea of me moving to another continent was not met with enthusiasm either.

But I was lucky; I had a supportive mom and stepdad who encouraged me to follow my dreams.

At 17, I applied to film school in Los Angeles and got in. The moment I turned 18, I packed my life—guarded by my parents until that point—into one suitcase and moved across the ocean.

Writing has always been my way of dealing with problems. When I was 20 and stuck in an emotionally abusive relationship, I wrote. When I lost my father to cancer the following year, I wrote. When I faced depression and mental breakdowns, I turned to writing.

I never considered myself a poet, but I have always been one. I wrote short poems about my feelings, which helped me process them. Despite being told I'd never be an author—or perhaps because of it—I've always wanted to write a book.
The pandemic provided the perfect opportunity to finish one I started in 2017, inspired by my life and struggles in Los Angeles.

I published it in 2021, around my 25th birthday, which was also when I began sharing my poetry online.
To my surprise, people seemed to resonate with what I had to say. I shared my day-to-day thoughts and gained increasing recognition for my work.

The years 2022 and 2023 have been difficult for me. While I've always experienced depressive and melancholic episodes, they had never been this intense. My home country was unexpectedly attacked, and I found myself glued to the news, hearing stories of people unable to reach their families. I cried for hours and struggled to sleep. Some days, I couldn't eat; others, I binge-ate. When I tried to sleep, nightmares would wake me up.

I tried to escape, as I had many times before when life became overwhelming. I sought comfort in movies and books, my go-to coping mechanism. Most days, I stayed in bed, binge-watching the same films and reading books. I would cry for a couple of hours, go to sleep, wake up from nightmares, and then repeat the cycle.

2024 has become a year for me to rediscover myself, to collect the pieces of Hanna and put them together. I started remembering who I was before and how I felt about things.
I began writing again—project idea after project idea, inspiration flowing freely. Then, while listening to a song, I felt inspired. I wrote a line about my father, expressing feelings I thought I had buried long ago. I started crying. I wrote another line about home, about friendship, about family and love. Letters were pouring out, and in them, I found healing. I was writing away my traumas, my pain, my anger, and my fears. I wrote for myself and those I love. Some of them have left me, and some have stayed with me forever. I wrote letters to them—my way of telling them that my story is not over. And it's not a tragic one. I wrote letters they will never read…

As I reflect on this journey, I hold onto the hope that my words will resonate with others. If this book helps at least one person feel seen, understood, or inspired, then my work will not be in vain.

Writing has always been my way of connecting with the world, and sharing my story is a way to extend a hand to those who may be navigating similar struggles. I believe that our experiences, no matter how painful, can serve as a beacon of hope for others, reminding them that they are not alone in their journey.

I

"Grief is the price we pay for love."

— Colin Murray Parkes

****

you are eight.
you just got your first roller skates.
riding with friends,
eating ice cream from McDonald's.
grandma makes borscht for lunch;
you eat it in the garden, laughing and gossiping.

you are eight.
you look out the window of your dad's old car
as he drives you to the beach.
in the evenings, you dance with your mama
to the music of Joe Dassin.
there is no war, no troubles, no fear.

you are eight.
the world has no boundaries.
you are completely free,
free to be yourself,
to be happy,
to be alive.

you are 27.
that world exists only in your memory.

THE DANCE OF NUMBNESS

you are numb in your bones, in your body.
numb in your soul and numb in your heart.
your world has just crumbled,
and you stand there in the ashes,
unsure of what comes next.

you have to keep moving.
you have to run, to dance, to laugh.
you can't stop.
because if you do, you will never move again.
if you stop laughing, you will drown in your own tears.
and so you continue.
you go out, you laugh, you dance.

you drink alcohol and you do a line:
anything to keep you going.
but even in the noisiest crowd,
the numbness catches up with you.
the laughter feels hollow, the dancing mechanical.
the drinks and lines offer only fleeting relief.
moments of oblivion vanish too quickly,
leaving you more exhausted than before.

you want to scream.
but you don't.
you can't.
they wouldn't understand.
so you keep the mask on.
you keep pretending.
you move, you dance, and you laugh.

people see the facade,
thinking you are coping and believing you are strong.
but inside, you're screaming for release,
for someone to see past the mask
and recognize your silent plea for help.
you hope one day to break free.
until then, you move, you dance, and you laugh.

Author's Note:

In 2018, I lost my dad to cancer. We hadn't seen each other for two years by that point. But he was planning to visit me in the U.S. that year for my birthday. By then, he had finally accepted that I was going on my own path. He underwent chemo and different treatments, and the doctors were optimistic. Then suddenly, his condition worsened, but he still didn't want me to worry or make the trip to Ukraine, claiming he would improve and visit the U.S. as planned. Two weeks later, he was gone.

I never got to say goodbye or make amends.

****

even when the sun was bright, my shadow stole all of light

****

they say cracks are how the light gets in.
there are probably no shadows inside of me left.

they say pain makes you stronger.
but I'd like to believe we don't have to be identified by it.

they say what is yours will find its way back to you,
but if it was mine,
why did it lose its path in the first place?

they say time heals all wounds.
but scars are left forever.

they say everything happens for a reason,
but sometimes the reason is hard to see.

they say you have to let go to be free,
but what if it feels like losing a part of myself?

they say trust is the foundation for everything,
yet it's so easily broken.

they say love conquers all….
they say…

LETTERS YOU WILL NEVER READ

****

and you wonder, will the world see you differently now?
little fatherless girl, with no one but herself to protect her.
will they know you are a fighter?
will they know you are a force?
or will they look and see only a little fatherless girl?

you often think back to how things used to be.
when the nights were filled with stories
and mornings with laughter.
you often think of the time when you knew you were safe.
when you knew he would guard your sleep
and keep the monsters out.

but you are no longer that child.
the innocent little girl he once loved.
you have known betrayal and heartbreak.
you have known grief and loss.
you learned that the only monsters we should fear
live deep inside us.
you learned to care for yourself and be strong.

little fatherless girl...

HANNA SHEBAR

****

the quiet is loud,
and my soul feels confined,
drifting in the night's endless ocean,
lost in the search for the calm
i am yet to find

HOME

some people are just lucky, i guess.
lucky they stayed in one place.
lucky their hearts were never split in two.
they belong.
they get to call one place home,
and they know where it is.

i wasn't so lucky.
i wandered and searched for roots
in the foreign soil, in borrowed time,
never finding what i left behind.

my home slipped through my fingers,
and i could never get it back.
the laughter of friends in familiar streets
felt like echoes from a dream i could not touch.
i stood on the edges of countless sunsets,
yearning for the colors that painted my past.
but all i found were shadows,
stretching longer than the days.

i wasn't so lucky.
what i called home doesn't exist.
it's a mirage fading with each passing year.
but perhaps home isn't a place after all.

maybe it's the laughter shared over late-night talks.
and the warmth of a hand held in silence.
and even the stories woven in the fabric of friendships

home might be the familiar scent of coffee brewing.
the rhythm of a favorite song that stirs the heart.
the comfort of knowing someone sees you,
even in the chaos of a world that feels unsteady.
perhaps home isn't a place after all.

LETTERS YOU WILL NEVER READ

****

perhaps in another lifetime things are different.
perhaps your family is always close by.
perhaps you are married and you have a child.
or perhaps, your daddy never left,
and your home is not broken.

perhaps in another lifetime there is no war.
there is no heartbreak.
perhaps you are even happy.
perhaps you work as a lawyer
and cook dinners for your husband.

perhaps in another lifetime the world is kind
and people are gentle with each other.
perhaps your dreams came true effortlessly
and your fears never found you.

perhaps in another lifetime love is simple and pure.
perhaps in another lifetime you didn't lose your friends,
and your grandma is still around.

perhaps in another lifetime everything you wished for
is just as it should be.

perhaps…

****

you broke my heart, but it's okay.
i've done it to myself a million times before.
i still do.
i overthink, romanticize, and over-love.
i build castles in the sky
and watch them crumble.
i give my all, wearing my heart on my sleeve.

but i've learned that tears are the rain that cleanse the soul.
i've learned there is strength in vulnerability.
i've learned that hope can rise from the deepest despair.
i've learned that love is a journey and not a destination.
and so i continue to overthink, romanticize, and over-love.

you broke my heart, but it's okay.
it needed breaking to know what true love really is
when it finally finds me.
each fracture teaches,
preparing my heart for love that is deep, pure, and right.

LETTERS YOU WILL NEVER READ

****

and there you are, learning that trust is easily broken.
learning that even the closest person can hurt you,
when in fact, the closest person is always the one
doing the most damage.
you will learn many more painful lessons along the way,
but that first one will always stay with you,
haunting and serving as a reminder
not to trust anyone again.

you were just a girl, but you learned.
you built walls around your heart,
hoping they would keep you safe from pain.
yet walls, no matter how strong, couldn't shield you.
they kept out the worst of the hurt
but also the best of the love.

with time, you will learn another lesson.
you will learn forgiveness, and you will forgive them—
not because they asked or apologized,
and not because they righted their wrong.
you will forgive, not for them, but for yourself.
you will learn there is peace in letting go.

and then, there you will be,
tearing down walls and healing wounds they left behind.
no longer defined by the hurt of the past, but shaped by it.
ready to embrace the future.

****

her daddy left but she still looks for him in every man.
yearning for the love that won't vanish like morning dew.
she crafts stories of redemption,
where every kind word is a chance
to heal the wounds he left.

with time she'll learn to see her own reflection,
not through the lens of abandonment,
but through the clarity of her resilience.
she will find that the love she so desperately wants
isn't in the shadows of the past but within herself.

she will find the courage to let go of the search.
and she will finally understand that her journey is her own,
and her heart, whole and unbroken, is enough!

LETTERS YOU WILL NEVER READ

****

some days it will hurt more.
some days you will feel like giving up,
like the world is on your shoulders
and you can't go on anymore.
some days you will cry, and curse,
and wish things were different.

but others you will find moments of hope.
some days you will laugh and feel lighter.
some days will show you the beauty of the small things,
and some days you will remember your own strength.

other days it will feel like a never-ending storm.
you will find yourself lost and alone.
you will feel angry and overwhelmed,
and you will wonder if the storm will ever end.

others you will know that it will,
that it is only darkest before dawn.
some days will be full of light and happiness,
and some nights will be full of heartache and tears.
some days will bring you joy and others sorrows.

but they all will have one thing in common:
through every shadow and sunrise, you grow,
and in the ebb and flow, you find your own story.

****

be gentle with yourself.

not everything will go according to plan,
not everything will be the way you want.
people will hurt you, and you will hurt them back.
life can get messy, chaotic, unpredictable.
all you can do is keep moving forward.
embrace the imperfections, learn from the setbacks,
and strive to grow. treat yourself with kindness
and patience, understanding that mistakes and
challenges are part of the journey.
focus on progress rather than perfection.

be gentle.
with others and YOURSELF

LETTERS YOU WILL NEVER READ

****

what if it was always meant to be this way?
what if everything you went through
was just another milestone in the process?
what if you had to endure
to find happiness on the other side?

i often wonder.
i wonder how things would have played out
if i had taken a different path, made a different choice.
would i still have made it here,
or would my life be unrecognizable?
would i still be pondering the same questions,
or would i have found answers long ago?

sometimes it feels like every challenge, every heartbreak,
was steering me towards this very moment,
as if there was an unseen force guiding me.
other times, it seems like a random series of events,
and i'm just trying to find meaning in the chaos.

i wonder, do we shape our destiny,
or does it shape us?

****

i'm sorry i can't fake it.
i'm sorry you think i'm rude when i'm being honest.
i'm sorry i can't smile when i feel like crying.
i'm sorry i can't fake it.

you say i'm mean, but i'm true.
i'm sorry my truth hurts you.
i'm sorry my honesty cuts deep.
i'm sorry i can't pretend to be someone i'm not.
i'm sorry i can't fake it.

you say i'm harsh, but i'm real.
i'm sorry i can't wear a mask to make you comfortable.
i'm sorry my rawness is too much for you to handle.
i'm sorry my emotions spill over, unfiltered and intense.
i'm sorry i can't fake it.

you say i'm too much, but i'm just enough for me.

RED BICYCLE

on my red bicycle,
rushing through the streets,
with the wind in my face.
the whole world was mine,
and the only trouble i knew
was how long till school starts again.

my grandma would bring cut-up fruits as a snack—
that was her love language.
my grandpa would spoil me with gifts.
home smelled of herbs and love.
i watched *Zorro* as i played with my Barbies,
while my mom cooked dinner.

my purple bicycle is waiting by the door,
never ridden.
the streets grew quiet and the wind grew colder.
i peel my own fruits and eat them uncut,
order takeout, and buy my own gifts.
home smells of hope but never of love.
the echoes of laughter have faded,
replaced by the hum of daily routines.

sometimes i think back to my red bicycle
and my rides through the streets,
but all i've got now is the purple one by the door,
never ridden.

****

somewhere between then and now,
i lost sight of myself.
i forgot who i was,
and i don't know who i am supposed to be.
i search, i look, and i copy,
hoping to get a glimpse of that girl i once knew.
but i don't recognize her anymore.
she is a stranger, a ghost, a fragment of the past.

somewhere between then and now,
i lost the person i was
in the pursuit of a person others wanted me to be.
i walked a path that wasn't mine,
guided by voices that weren't my own.

somewhere between now and then,
i will find the courage to reclaim myself.
i will remember who i was
and discover who i am meant to be.
i will search, look, and explore,
hoping to catch a glimpse of the girl i once knew.
she may feel like a stranger, a ghost, a fragment of the past,
but i will learn to recognize her again.
i will walk my own path, guided by my own voice.

somewhere between now and then,
i will find myself again.

****

it's okay to outgrow people.
even the ones you love.
or perhaps especially the ones you love.

life moves fast.
seasons change, feelings change,
people come together and people grow apart.
the only thing constant in this world is change itself.

it may hurt and you may find it difficult to accept,
but sometimes the best you can do for yourself
is leave behind what no longer serves you.

growth can be painful,
but through this pain we find our strength.
every ending is the new beginning.
and even when one chapter is over,
you are the one holding the pen to write what comes next.

HANNA SHEBAR

****

no matter how fast i run,
i always find my way back.
you can't outrun your pain.

no matter how much i try,
i always end up facing the shadows
i thought i left behind.
you can't escape what lives within you.

LETTERS YOU WILL NEVER READ

****

i am my mother's favorite daughter.
don't mind that she only has one.
people say we are one and the same,
perhaps with a little more rage.

i am my mother's favorite daughter.
she braided my hair and told me stories before bed.
she taught me to be kind, to be honest and true,
to love people and the world.

i am my mother's favorite daughter.
for me, she broke the chains of anger.
she crumbled generational curses
and stopped the cycle of pain, taking it all for herself.
she faced the legacy of women who were silenced
and made sure that was never my story.

i am my mother's favorite daughter.
she is me, and i am her.

II

"Although the world is full of suffering,
it is also full of the overcoming of it."

— Helen Keller

HANNA SHEBAR

****

we are more than our pain.
more than our scars.
more than our mistakes.
more than our losses.
more than our regrets.
we are more than our failures.
and we are more than our past.

we are in the present.
curving our future with every breath we take.
we are the strength in our resilience.
we are hope in our dreams.
and we are the love in our hearts.

we are the light in the darkness,
the calm in the storm.
we are the laughter amidst the tears,
and the courage in the face of fear.

we are the sum of all our experiences,
but we are not defined by any single one.

****

the moment comes when you realize
you can't carry that anger any longer.
you can't live with bitterness in your heart
and tears in your eyes.

the moment comes when you know
you have to let go.
you have to forgive them.
you realize it wasn't their fault
they didn't give you what you needed.
how could they when they never had it themselves?
they loved you the best they knew how.

they left a hole in your heart,
but the only way to make it smaller is to let go.
the pain might never go away,
but it will get less noticeable.

the moment comes when you realize
it wasn't their fault any more than it was yours.
and you find peace in it.

****

forgive that version of yourself
that didn't know any better.
the scared, the judgmental, the insecure,
the anxious, the unloved.
she did what she thought she had to.
she did what she thought was right.

forgive that version of yourself
that thought she'd never be enough.
she was doing the best she could
with what she knew and what she had.

forgive her, and love her, because she hasn't.
she carried burdens too heavy,
and felt wounds too deep.
fought battles unseen,
and cried silent tears in the night.

forgive that version of yourself
that felt lost in the darkness
and couldn't see the light.
the one who questioned her worth
and doubted her dreams.
the one who didn't believe in her strength.

forgive her.
because she hadn't forgiven herself.
forgive her and set her free.

****

the truth is, life doesn't slow down for anyone.
you can't put it on pause or on hold,
and even if you try,
it will catch up with you eventually.

life is not a game of Sims
where you can exit without saving
and try again tomorrow.
you have to own your mistakes,
learn from them, and move forward.

the truth is, we are all going in blind,
learning in real time.
we stumble, we fall, we get back up.

the truth is, there isn't a manual for this journey,
no set paths or guaranteed outcomes.
the truth is, life doesn't slow down for anyone.
all we can do is live it.

ONE DAY

i know one day it will get easier.
you will stop crying yourself to sleep every night,
and not because it won't hurt anymore
but because it will hurt less.

i know one day you will realize life is not all bad.
and even the pain can be a blessing.

i know one day you will laugh again.
and you will find joy in little moments.

i know one day you will finally choose yourself:
your happiness, your peace, your beautiful heart.

and i know one day you will find love.
first in yourself and then in another.

one day!

****

not every story needs to have a happy ending.
sometimes an ending is more than enough.
sometimes it's about the lessons learned along the way
rather than the destination itself.

sometimes the only resolution is acceptance.
sometimes it's about recognizing
that not all tales wrap up neatly,
but every experience shapes who we become.

not every story needs to have a happy ending.
sometimes an ending is more than enough.

****

at the end of the day,
we were never meant to be unhappy.
life was always for living.
life was always for loving, for laughing,
for gazing at the stars, for dreaming.
it was always for dancing to your favorite tune,
for eating fruits by the sea, and for hugging your friends.

at the end of the day,
we were never meant to be unhappy.
to wage wars, to hurt each other, and to hate ourselves.
life was always for finding joy in little things,
for building bridges between hearts,
for sharing stories, and for holding hands.
life was always for cherishing sunrises.

at the end of the day,
we were never meant to be unhappy…

****

just because they couldn't love you the way you needed
doesn't mean no one else will.
just because they couldn't be the person for you
doesn't mean no one else will.
their inability to give you their best
doesn't make you undeserving of it.

HANNA SHEBAR

****

i'm still learning what life is.
is it a kiss in the morning?
or the hug of goodbye?
perhaps it's the silence shared with a loved one.
maybe it's even the laughter over an old joke.
or perhaps it's the tears you shed
when no one's watching.
maybe it's the dreams we chase, never quite catching.

i'm still learning what life is.

****

they told me not to trust easily,
but i didn't listen.
they told me not to wear my heart on my sleeve,
but i didn't know any other way.
they told me to keep my guard up,
but i ignored them.
they told me to be cautious,
but i was too busy believing in the good.
they told me the world was cruel,
but i chose to see the light in every shadow.
they told me to toughen up,
but i couldn't change my gentle nature.

now, i carry the scars of my trust,
the weight of my open heart,
and the pain of lowered guards.

let them call me a fool.
let them say i was naive.
let them laugh at my gentleness.
i'll keep trusting.
i'll keep loving.
i'll keep believing in the good,
for that's the only way i know how to live.

****

and i'll forever wish i could go back in time.
not to change things but to feel them again.

****

i broke my own heart.
and then i healed it.
i pulled myself from the darkness time after time.
i stopped counting.
i was there when no one else would show up for me.
i held myself as i cried,
and i promised it would get better.

i learned to be my own savior.
i learned to be gentle with myself,
to forgive missteps and celebrate the small victories.

i became my own hero and keeper of my dreams.
i gathered the broken pieces of my heart
and mended them with threads of hope.

now, i stand tall,
not because i never fell,
but because i rose every time i did.

HANNA SHEBAR

****

can we trust our memory?
was the past really better than the present?
or is our mind playing tricks on us?
do we really remember things and people
for what and who they were,
or do we remember them the way we hoped they would be?

in the haze of yesterday,
do we see through rose-tinted lenses,
repainting faded hues with regret?
we clutch at fragments,
looking through a mosaic of illusions and reality,
piecing together nostalgia and idealism.

in the end,
can we really trust our memory?

****

today i cried again.
i didn't cry over you.
no, i don't do that anymore.
now i cry for the girl i used to be back then.
i cry for the naivety i once knew.
i cry for the person i was.

i cry for the dreams that were shattered
and promises that were broken.
for the nights spent awake
and for the days spent pretending i was fine.
i cry for the love i so freely gave,
not knowing it would be taken for granted.

those are not sad tears.
i don't shed those anymore.
i cry for my strength, for my courage.
i cry for my wisdom and my heart.
i cry tears of gratitude, not sorrow.

i cry for the woman i have become.
and i cry for the future.

HANNA SHEBAR

****

no one knows what the future holds.
in a heartbeat, stories are told.
lives intertwined, people brought together
and people torn apart.
one second can spark a dream,
and one second can shatter hope.

no one knows what the future holds.
but it is in the unknown we can find our way.
through joy and through sorrow,
through loss and through pain.

one second is enough to fall in love,
but also fall out of it.
one second is enough to lose someone dear,
but also to meet the one who will change your world forever.

no one knows what the future holds.
it's still unwritten, and that is the beauty of it.

****

letting go doesn't mean giving up,
but rather accepting that not everything is meant to be.
not everyone is meant to be your friend.
not every event is yours to experience.

sometimes paths diverge,
not out of failure or lack of trying,
but because the universe has a different plan—
a plan that may be unseen, unfelt, or misunderstood
until the moment when letting go turns into letting in.

letting in the truth that some chapters end
so others can begin.
letting in the peace that comes with release,
knowing that what was, was necessary,
but what's to come is just as vital.

and in that space,
between holding on and moving forward,
you find yourself, not lost, but liberated,
ready to embrace what's next
with open arms and an open heart.

****

i promise, it will get better.
even if it doesn't feel like it.
i promise you will laugh again.
you will know joy and you will see the beauty of life.

i promise i'll listen.
i'll be patient even though i'm not known for it.
i promise i will be your anchor in the storm
and your light in the darkness.

i promise i will wash away your tears.
i promise i will be your strength when you feel weak,
i will be your voice when words escape you.

i promise i will believe in you,
and i will cherish your dreams and fight for them.

i promise i will be here,
even when you don't ask me to, especially then.
i will hold you and I will lend you my shoulder.

i promise…

To me, from me

LETTERS YOU WILL NEVER READ

****

you will wake up one morning and know peace.
the day will be bright again.
the wind will play with your hair,
and life will feel like a gentle kiss.

your heart will be filled with hope,
and your world will be filled with happiness.
each moment will be a chance to breathe,
to dream, to smile without reason,
and to simply be alive.

you'll find joy in the things
like the warmth of the sun on your face
and the sound of birds singing.
you will learn to live here and now
and be grateful for each day.

you will wake up one morning,
and you will be ready.
ready to heal, ready to laugh, to dance, to learn,
and ready to live your beautiful life.

III

"Keep your face always toward
the sunshine—and shadows will fall behind you."

— *Walt Whitman*

HANNA SHEBAR

****

i was made to eat strawberries,
to live by the ocean,
read books, and to walk underneath the trees.

i was made to dance in the rain,
to bake cookies,
and to laugh until my stomach hurt.

i was made to feel deeply,
give my heart fully,
and to cherish moments.

i was made to explore the world,
to tell stories,
and create memories with the people i love.

****

love is a pat on the back.
love is a "text me when you get home."
love is a cup of tea on a cold day.
love is a hug.
love is answering a phone call in the middle of the night.
love is sharing a laugh over a silly joke
only the two of you understand.
love is growing together.
love is remembering the little things.
love is a gentle touch that says, "i'm here."
love is forgiveness.
love is understanding.
love is being seen.
love is the comfort of silence.
love is a smile that brightens your day.
love is different and yet the same.

****

you will have bad days,
and you will have good days,
and then the bad ones again.

life is all of them,
and also something in between.
you will feel uncertain about what comes next,
often caught between hope and doubt.

but each day is a new chance
to find meaning,
to embrace the highs and endure the lows.

remember that it's okay to not have all the answers,
and that each moment, whether good or bad,
contributes to the journey that shapes who you are.

****

i'm the thinker of tender thoughts.
i'm a dreamer, a lover, a poet.
i am a woman.

in the dance of shadows and light,
i find strength in my vulnerabilities.
i am a symphony of courage wrapped in gentleness.
i am a woman.

i am the echo of ancient songs,
the keeper of forgotten promises,
a soul that dares to love deeply.

i am a woman,
and my heart beats to the rhythm of dreams.

****

i taught myself forgiveness.
i have learned that people aren't there to get you;
they aren't trying to hurt you.
people aren't bad, not really.
we hurt each other because we don't know any better.
we act from our wounds, unaware of the pain we carry.
we lash out, not realizing that we're all just searching
for connection and understanding.

i learned that forgiveness isn't about excusing the hurt;
it's about releasing the hold it has on us.

****

good things don't always last forever,
but that's okay, because neither do bad things.
and that's what makes life so truly beautiful.
moments come, and moments go,
just like waves in the ocean.
each one a chance to learn, to feel, or to grow.
for every sunset leads to a brand new dawn.

HANNA SHEBAR

****

the world isn't all bad.
people aren't all evil.
it isn't all fighting and it isn't all anger.
there are good things too.
there is kindness in this world as well.
there is beauty. and there is art. and music.
there are those who believe. and who create.
and those who inspire. and even those who love.

yes, the world isn't all bad.

LETTERS YOU WILL NEVER READ

****

one lifetime isn't enough.
how am i to open a café in Paris,
to make art in Berlin,
to surf on the coast of California,
to write books in the Scottish cottage?
to pick wildflowers in the Crimean mountains,
to eat pizza in Tuscany,
and to ride my bike through the streets of Amsterdam?

one lifetime isn't enough.
it isn't enough to laugh at the corny jokes your dad makes.
it isn't enough to enjoy all the sunsets with friends.
it isn't enough to explore the depths of our passions,
and it isn't enough to experience the richness of your love.

one lifetime isn't enough.
but that's all we have, so it will have to do.

****

we are the echoes of all the love we've ever given.
we are the whispers of every heart we've touched.
and we are the silent prayers for those we've cherished.

****

magic is real. i've seen it.
it's in the meal your mom prepares for you
that makes your day a little easier.
it's in the joke your friend cracks.
it's in the eyes that look at you with love.
it's in the light playing with water.
it's in the wind creating music.
it's in the sky and in the trees.
it's in the warmth of a hug.
it's in the unexpected kindness from a stranger.
it's in the moments that make you feel alive.

magic is real.
you just need to know where to look.

****

to be a woman.
to be a woman is to have a heart
big enough to fill the whole world in.
it's to carry love in it even when it's cracked.
it's to have your father's rage and your mom's impatience.

to be a woman
is to see the best in people.
it's to cherish the small moments,
the fleeting glances, the unsaid words.
to be a woman is to turn chaos into calm
and back into chaos.
it's to hold the world together
with invisible threads of strength and tenderness.
it's to fight battles unseen
and wear scars like jewelry.

to be a woman
is to love fiercely and forgive deeply.
to be a woman is to nurture dreams—
both your own and those of others.
it's to prove to the world that you can,
even when they tell you it's impossible.

oh, to be a woman!

LETTERS YOU WILL NEVER READ

****

it might be hard to believe,
but one day you will miss this.
you will be in the kitchen making lunch for your kids,
and a song will come up on your playlist.

and then you will be back.
back when life was simpler.
when you were free.
back to the times when you danced till the sunrise
and slept till sunset.

when you gave your love easily,
without asking for anything in return.
it will bring you back right here,
where you complain how hard life is,
wanting to go back to when it was easier.

you will miss the carefree times and late-night talks.
the smell of cigarettes and the taste of cheap vodka.
you will remember the warm summer nights
under the stars you shared with those
who understood you best.

there you will be,
in your kitchen, making lunch for your kids,
thinking how great those times were.

****

maybe in another universe none of this has happened to you.
you have stayed whole and safe,
and you never learned the taste of betrayal.
in another universe, you aren't from a broken home.
in another universe, you never left your little bubble.
in another universe, summer never ends.
you are still there,
living by the sea and eating borscht for lunch.

maybe in another universe.

but you live in this one, where seasons change.
where you get to fall, get up, fall again,
and then lift others up with you.
in this universe, you've known pain.
you've tasted the ashes of trust burning in your mouth,
and you've learned to accept, forgive, and love.
in this universe, you mended
and built a safe home for yourself.
in this universe, you burst your horizons,
never to be confined to one place again.
in this universe, you found strength in the cracks
and beauty in brokenness.

in this universe.

****

and then you realize
there is nowhere you'd rather be than today.
you dwell on the past,
but given the choice, you'd pick the present.
with all its hardships and heartbreak,
with all its pain and imperfections.

and then you realize
the past is just a beautiful picture
painted with nostalgia.
you realize the present is the only real thing left.
it is a bare canvas on which you can still paint.
it is the story that hasn't been told yet.

and then you realize
the present is a gift.
each moment fleeting, each breath a chance.
the now is YOURS.

****

thank you for today.
thank you for the sunrise and the alarm in the morning.
thank you for calling my name.
thank you for the smell of coffee.
thank you for telling me about your day
and for listening to my never-ending stories.

thank you for making me smile.
thank you for all the little arguments we have
and for letting me be myself.
thank you for all the times you hold me,
and for all the moments you made me feel seen.

thank you for the sunsets,
and for the rainy days.
for all the cold nights and the warm hugs.
thank you for the tears and the laughter.
for the walks and the moments of silence.

and if tomorrow doesn't come,
thank you for today…

We are all traveling through life together, facing similar challenges. Some are universal, while others are unique to us. Life can be both beautiful and terrifying at times. We all learn heartache and loss. The world teaches us to live through grief as well as through happiness. We hold grudges, and we learn how to be kinder. We forgive, and we love.

We keep walking, together yet apart, finding our way through the messiness of being human. We discover who we are in the quiet moments, learn how to listen to the whispers of our hearts, and find peace in the uncertainty.

And in this journey, we learn that not everything finds closure. We learn there are things left unsaid, stories that remain unfinished — letters you will never read.

But even without closure, there is healing.
We heal by writing new chapters, by speaking the words
we once kept hidden, by opening ourselves to love again
even after our hearts have been broken.
We learn that not every story needs an ending to be complete.

ACKNOWLEDGMENTS

First and foremost, I want to thank my mom, for being my number one supporter since day one. Thank you for always believing in me and encouraging me to dream. And to my stepdad, thank you for not being just a stepdad, but a dad who stepped in.

To my dear friend Golsa, thank you for always hyping me up and reminding me of my own strength.

To all the beautiful people I am fortunate to have in my life—thank you for helping me discover myself and for celebrating who I am.

And finally, to you, my reader—thank you for all the love and support you have shown me through the years.

www.ingramcontent.com/pod-product-compliance
Lightning Source LLC
Chambersburg PA
CBHW020547080526
44583CB00013B/1031